JUV/
KF
228
.S27
J36
1998

SCOTTS

Chicago Public Library

R0127277823

The Dred Scott decision.

P9-EFH-815

SEP   1998

CHICAGO PUBLIC LIBRARY
SCOTTSDALE BRANCH
4101 W. 79TH ST.   60652

Cornerstones of Freedom

The Dred Scott Decision

Brendan January

CHILDREN'S PRESS®
A Division of Grolier Publishing
New York • London • Hong Kong • Sydney
Danbury, Connecticut

Eliza and Lizzie,
children of Dred Scott

Library of Congress Cataloging-in-Publication Data

January, Brendan, 1972–
    The Dred Scott decision / by Brendan January.
        p. cm.—(Cornerstones of freedom)
    Includes index.
    Summary: Places the events relating to the 1857 Supreme Court
decision regarding rights of slaves into the larger context of the
conflict about slavery among the states.
    ISBN: 0-516-20833-0 (lib. bdg.)   0-516-26457-5 (pbk)
    1. Scott, Dred, 1809–1858—Trials, litigation, etc.—Juvenile
literature. 2. Slavery—Law and legislation—United States—Juvenile
literature. 3. Slavery—United States—Legal status of slaves in free
states—Juvenile literature. [1. Scott, Dred, 1809–1858. 2. Slavery—
Law and legislation.] I. Title. II. Series.
KF228.S27J36 1998
342.73'087—dc21
                                            97-11713
                                                 CIP
                                                 AC

©1998 Children's Press®, a Division of Grolier Publishing Co., Inc.
All rights reserved. Published simultaneously in Canada.
Printed in the United States of America.
1 2 3 4 5 6 7 8 9 10 R 07 06 05 04 03 02 01 00 99 98

CHICAGO PUBLIC LIBRARY
SCOTTSDALE BRANCH
4101 W. 79TH ST.   60652

On April 6, 1846, a black slave named Dred Scott asked a Missouri court to give him his freedom. Scott claimed that he was free because his owner had taken him to live in a state and a territory where slavery was illegal. After eleven years of delays, Scott's case arrived at the highest court in the United States— the Supreme Court in Washington, D.C. By that time, however, the case represented more than just one slave's attempt to win freedom. It drew the attention of the entire nation. The issues being debated were at the center of a struggle that was pulling the United States apart. The cause of this struggle was slavery.

Dred Scott

In the early 1800s, slavery began to divide the United States. In the North, laborers worked in bustling factories and on farms. Cities swelled in size and new railroads cut through the country-side. In the South, giant plantations and small farms dotted the landscape. The southern economy depended on slaves to harvest crops such as cotton. Without slavery, southerners feared their way of life would collapse.

Above: Northern towns grew quickly as more people began to work in factories. Below: Plantation owners considered slave labor necessary for the success of the southern economy.

In 1819, the members of the U.S. Congress debated whether to allow slavery in the

unsettled territories just west of the Mississippi River. Congressmen from the northern states wanted to reserve the land for free farmers. Congressmen from the southern states demanded that the territories be opened to slave owners. In 1820, Congress decided to divide the territories into two sections. In the northern section, Congress banned slavery. In the southern section, Congress permitted it. This deal, called the Missouri Compromise, satisfied almost everyone. The nation grew peacefully for the next twenty-eight years.

The Missouri Compromise was devised to satisfy northerners, who did not want slavery to spread outside the South. It was also meant to please southerners, who believed that slavery should be allowed to flourish in other territories.

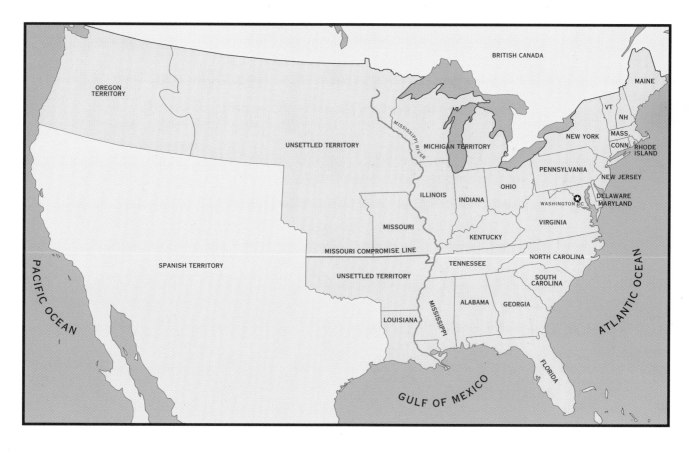

Antislavery gatherings were common in the North, where most people agreed that slavery was wrong.

In the late 1840s and 1850s, however, the slavery controversy resurfaced. Abolitionists (people who wanted to abolish, or end, slavery) began to call slavery unfair and cruel. Outraged southerners defended their right to own slaves. Slaves were considered to be property, and the right to own property had been established in the U.S. Constitution. How, the slave owners asked, can Congress abolish slavery in the territories? Many slave owners demanded the right to establish slavery wherever they wanted.

In 1854, a group of northerners formed a new political party, called the Republicans, to oppose the pro-slavery southerners. The Republicans did not suggest abolishing slavery where it already existed. But they did insist that slavery be banned from the unsettled western territories. These lands, the Republicans declared, should be reserved for free farmers, not slavery.

Throughout the 1850s, Republican congressmen and southern congressmen bitterly debated the future of slavery in the territories. Many people feared the issue could destroy the Union. Some politicians hoped that the Supreme Court would solve the problem. Protected from the angry mood in Congress, the Supreme Court could settle the slavery dispute with one final decision. The opportunity arrived when Dred Scott's case was brought before the Court in 1854.

Congressional debates over slavery became so heated that violence sometimes erupted.

Slave auctions were held to sell slaves from one owner to another.

Dred Scott's journey to the Supreme Court was long and complicated. He was born into slavery in Virginia sometime around 1800. (The births and deaths of slaves were often unrecorded.) In 1830, Dred Scott and his owner, Peter Blow, settled in Missouri. Soon after, either Blow or his daughter sold Dred to a U.S. army doctor named John Emerson. Scott lived with Dr. Emerson in St. Louis, Missouri, until 1834, when Emerson moved to Fort Armstrong in

Fort Armstrong, Illinois, was built along the Mississippi River.

Illinois. Dred went to Fort Armstrong with Dr. Emerson. For two years, they lived a quiet life in the fort. Emerson, however, grew tired of the post. He sent several letters to the United States War Department asking for a new assignment.

In 1836, the War Department transferred Emerson to Fort Snelling in the Wisconsin Territory. Scott accompanied him. Wisconsin was not yet a state, and the region was largely unsettled. To Emerson, Fort Snelling was even more lonely than Fort Armstrong. After only a year in the Wisconsin Territory, Emerson complained of poor health and asked to leave.

Dred Scott's case
also requested
freedom for his
wife Harriet
(right), and their
two children, Eliza
and Lizzie.

In 1837, after sending several letters of
complaint to the War Department, Emerson
was transferred to a fort in Louisiana. There,
Emerson met and married Eliza Sanford. Soon
after, Dr. Emerson, Eliza, and Dred Scott
returned to Fort Snelling in the Wisconsin
Territory. In 1842, Emerson finally decided to
settle in St. Louis, where he died on December
29, 1843. In his will, Emerson left Dred and
Dred's wife, Harriet, to Eliza Emerson.

Almost three years later, on April 6, 1846, Dred and Harriet Scott petitioned, or asked, a Missouri court for their freedom. Dred Scott stated that he and his wife were being held illegally as slaves. Scott claimed that he should be free because he had lived for two years in Illinois, a free state. Scott pointed out that he had also lived in the Wisconsin Territory, where slavery was banned by the 1820 Missouri Compromise.

It is unclear exactly how Dred Scott began his quest for freedom. He could not read or write, and he signed his name with only a simple mark. No detailed descriptions of him exist, although one newspaper article described him as "being not more than five feet six inches [167 centimeters] high." And there is only one known photograph of him. Another newspaper described Dred as "illiterate, but not ignorant," and possessing a "strong common sense." Dred Scott did receive help from sympathetic lawyers, but no one is sure how much help he received. It is clear, however, that Scott was a man who desperately wanted his freedom. He battled for years in his attempt to win his case.

Hamilton Gamble, who may have been one of Dred Scott's legal advisors

The Missouri state court accepted Scott's request for a hearing and set a date for the trial, which began on June 30, 1847. Dred and Harriet believed they would be granted their freedom because an agreement existed among the free states and the slave states called "state comity." This meant that southern courts agreed to free any slaves who had lived in a free state for a long period of time. In return, northern courts agreed not to free slaves who were only traveling through a free state with their owners. Dred and his wife had lived for more than two years in Illinois—a free state. They expected the Missouri court to rule in their favor. In 1850, after more than two years of complicated arguments, the jury hearing the Scotts' case awarded them their freedom. Mrs. Emerson appealed the decision (asked that the case be reheard in a higher court). In 1852, the case was heard in the highest court in Missouri.

By 1852, however, the United States had changed drastically. Northerners and southerners were bitterly divided over the issue of slavery. Several northern courts had ignored the state comity agreement and freed slaves as soon as they stepped on northern soil. Judge William Scott (who was not related to Dred Scott) was the Missouri supreme court justice who ruled on Eliza Emerson's appeal. Judge Scott resented the northern courts and the abolitionists. He was

Dred and Harriet Scott lived in the free state of Illinois for more than two years. They believed the Missouri court would free them.

❶ *1800(?): Dred Scott is born into slavery in Virginia.*

❷ *1830: Dred settles in St. Louis, Missouri, with owner, Peter Blow.*

  1832: Dred is sold to John Emerson.

❸ *1834: Dred goes to Fort Armstrong, Illinois, with Emerson.*

❹ *1836: Dred moves to Fort Snelling, Wisconsin Territory, with Emerson.*

  1837: Dred stays at Fort Snelling while Emerson goes to Louisiana.

  1838: Emerson returns to Fort Snelling.

❺ *1840: Dred goes back to St. Louis with Eliza Emerson; John Emerson travels to Florida.*

  1842: Emerson returns to St. Louis.

  1843: Emerson dies; Eliza becomes Dred's owner.

determined to defend the rights of slave owners. The judge ruled that Missouri did not have to obey the laws of other states. The Illinois laws granting freedom to slaves who had lived in that state for a long time could therefore be ignored. According to Judge Scott's ruling, Dred and Harriet became slaves again when they returned to Missouri soil. The judge overturned the first court's decision. Dred and Harriet's quest for freedom had been crushed.

Antislavery and pro-slavery groups were so determined to defeat each other that riots sometimes broke out between the two sides. This riot took place in Alton, Illinois.

Soon after, Dred Scott was contacted by Roswell M. Field, a Vermonter who had settled in St. Louis. Field hated slavery, and he hoped to use the Scotts' case to attack the laws that protected it. Dred, however, was no longer owned by Eliza Emerson. She had remarried and moved to Massachusetts. She had given Dred to her brother, John Sanford, who lived in New York.

Field told Dred Scott that John Sanford could be sued because New York was a free state. Cases between citizens of different states were heard in United States federal courts. Federal

Roswell Field, born and raised in the free state of Vermont, was determined to help Dred Scott sue his new owner, John Sanford.

courts and state courts had different responsibilities. State courts enforced the laws that existed within the state's borders. Federal courts ruled on the laws that existed among the states in the Union. Since Eliza Emerson and Dred Scott both lived in Missouri, Dred's case could only be heard in Missouri courts. But now that the citizens of two different states (Scott of Missouri and Sanford of New York) were involved, Roswell Field believed that Scott could win his case in the federal court.

On November 2, 1853, Roswell Field filed suit in a U.S. federal court for Dred Scott's freedom. The fact that Scott's case would be heard in a federal court increased its importance. Decisions made in federal courts affect every state in the Union.

The first trial was unsuccessful. The court declared that Scott was still a slave by Missouri law. The unfavorable decision left Scott with one last chance—the Supreme Court of the United States. Field wrote to Montgomery Blair, a prominent Republican lawyer in Washington, D.C. Blair had experience arguing in front of the Supreme Court, and he agreed to take Dred's case. Sanford hired a tough pro-slavery lawyer, Henry Geyer, to argue his side of the case. The case was accepted as *Dred Scott v. Sandford* (the court reporter misspelled Sanford's name and it was never corrected).

The U.S. Supreme Court was led by Chief Justice Roger B. Taney. Born and raised in the slave state of Maryland, Taney regarded black people as inferior to white people. He viewed the antislavery movement with fear and alarm, and he believed abolitionists were dangerous radicals intent on destroying the rights of southerners. Taney hoped to use the Dred Scott case to strengthen slavery. Most of the other eight justices on the court shared Taney's beliefs. Four of them came from the South, and

Montgomery Blair argued Dred Scott's case in front of the U.S. Supreme Court.

they all held slavery as an important right that was protected by the Constitution. The other four justices were from northern states, but two of them were sympathetic to slavery.

Chief Justice Roger Taney, born in 1777, was determined to protect the rights of slave owners.

Dred Scott's case was scheduled to begin on February 11, 1856, in the Supreme Court in Washington, D.C. At that time, the Court was located in the basement of the Capitol. The nine justices, clothed in long black robes, sat in a row behind a long table at the head of the courtroom.

As the arguments began, important questions emerged: What does it mean to be a citizen? A citizen is a member of a country or a state. A citizen can testify in court and is protected by the law. Can a slave be a citizen? Blair argued that Dred Scott was a citizen, so he had rights guaranteed by the Constitution. Geyer responded

Dred Scott's case was argued in the old Supreme Court chamber in the Capitol. Today, this chamber is preserved and the court meets in its own, separate building.

that slaves were not citizens, and that Scott had no right to be in the Supreme Court.

The arguments dragged on for days. When the arguments were completed, the justices debated the details of the case in their private chambers. Finally, on May 12, 1856, the justices decided to hear the arguments again on December 15. The case had attracted the attention of several groups throughout the country. The arguments over Dred Scott's future were also at the center of heated debates between northerners and southerners. Republicans, slaveholders, and abolitionists all understood that the Court's decision would have a serious impact on slavery and its future in the United States.

As the Dred Scott case drew more attention from the public, supporters from both sides sometimes argued so intensely that fights resulted.

On December 15, 1856, reporters and politicians crowded into the courtroom to hear the arguments. Again, the question of whether Dred Scott was a citizen arose. Montgomery Blair continued to argue that Scott was a citizen. Although black people had no rights in many states, some states (such as Massachusetts) gave free black people rights as citizens. If the state of Massachusetts recognized blacks as citizens, so should the United States government.

In Henry Geyer's response to Blair, Geyer stated that Dred Scott, as a black person, was not a citizen. Non-citizens did not have the full protection of the law because the law was for white people only. Black people could not sue

The members of the 1856 U.S. Supreme Court who heard Dred Scott's case included (front row): Chief Justice Roger Taney (center), Peter Daniel (second from right), and Samuel Nelson (right). (Back row): Robert Grier (left), Benjamin Curtis (second from left), and John Campbell (third from left).

another person in court, nor could they argue against a white person in court.

In response to Geyer's argument, Blair decided to change tactics. He reminded the justices that Dred had lived in Illinois for two years. So, Blair asked, how could Dred Scott be a slave in a place where there was no slavery? Geyer replied that Dr. Emerson and Scott had simply traveled through Illinois because Emerson had no intention of living there. If Emerson had settled in Illinois, Geyer admitted, then Scott could rightfully claim his freedom. But Emerson returned to Missouri, and therefore, Scott remained a slave. Blair reminded the Court that Scott had also spent three years living in the Wisconsin Territory. As a result, Scott and his family should be free because the Missouri Compromise banned slavery from the Wisconsin Territory.

At that moment, Henry Geyer made a fateful decision. He decided to argue that Scott was not free in the Wisconsin Territory because the Missouri Compromise violated the Constitution. Geyer argued that the U.S. Congress had no right to restrict slavery from the territories. Slave owners had the right to settle with their slaves in any territory they chose. Geyer's argument changed the case. Instead of simply ruling on one slave's freedom, the Supreme Court could decide the future of slavery in all of the territories.

Spectators filled the courtroom to hear the arguments in Dred Scott v. Sandford.

In his reply to Geyer, Blair pointed out that Congress had banned slavery in other territories, and no one had declared that decision unconstitutional. According to Blair, Geyer was simply ignoring history. The arguments lasted for four days before they ended on December 19, 1856. Dred Scott, the lawyers, and the spectators would have to wait until the justices made a decision.

For three months, the nation waited while the nine justices argued among themselves. Was Dred Scott a citizen? Was the Missouri Compromise unconstitutional? Chief Justice Taney hoped to write a decision that would be supported by all of the justices on the Court. (Cases are decided by a majority vote.) Justice Taney convinced most of the justices to support his view of the case. With these justices in agreement, Taney wrote the Court's decision.

On March 6, 1857, the small courtroom was packed with reporters and spectators. Dred Scott, Montgomery Blair, and Henry Geyer stood silently as the justices entered the room and sat down. Exhausted from long hours of writing, Chief Justice Taney read the opinion in a weak and whispery voice. It took him more than two hours to read the fifty-five-page decision.

Geyer based his argument against the Missouri Compromise on the U.S. Constitution. Written in 1787, it provided the framework for our nation's laws.

Taney addressed the first question: Was Dred Scott a citizen? No, he answered. Taney explained that black people did not have the same rights as white people. The writers of the Declaration of Independence did not intend to include black people when they wrote "all men are created equal."

Taney addressed the next question: Was Dred Scott free because he lived in a territory where slavery was banned by the Missouri Compromise? No, Taney ruled, because the Missouri Compromise was a violation of the Constitution. Taney declared that Congress in 1820 had no right to establish the Missouri

The first African slaves arrived in North America in 1619. By the time of Dred Scott's case, slaves had been considered noncitizens for more than two hundred years.

Compromise. Taney reasoned that slaves were property, and the right to own property is guaranteed by the Constitution. Congress could not deny slave owners the right to take their slaves with them wherever they went.

Finally, Taney answered one last question: Was Dred Scott free because he lived in the free state of Illinois? No. Taney explained that Scott spent only a brief amount of time in Illinois. Since the laws of Illinois did not apply in the state of Missouri, Scott became a slave again as soon as he returned to Missouri.

Not all of the justices agreed with Taney's decision. Justice Benjamin Curtis wrote a separate decision, called a dissenting opinion. The next day (March 7), Justice Curtis read his opinion to the Court. He first argued that black people in several states in the Union possessed the rights of free citizens. Therefore, Taney's statement that black people were not citizens of the United States was wrong. Curtis then questioned Taney's decision that Congress could not ban slavery from the territories. Curtis argued that Congress had banned slavery from territories in the past. The Constitution gave Congress the right to make the laws within territories. Therefore, Curtis reasoned, the Missouri Compromise did not violate the Constitution. Dred Scott, Curtis concluded, should be free.

Benjamin Curtis, from Massachusetts, believed that Dred Scott should be free.

The owners of plantations, such as this one in Georgia, were pleased by the Court's ruling, which ensured that their slavery-based economy would continue.

Justice Curtis's opinion, however, could not outweigh the other justices who supported Taney. Within weeks, Taney's opinion was printed in newspapers across the country. In the South, slave owners were thrilled that the Missouri Compromise no longer legally existed. The *Louisville* (KY) *Democrat* declared, "the decision is right, and the argument unanswerable." The *Constitutionalist* bragged, "Southern opinion upon the subject of slavery . . . is now the law of the land." Other newspapers stated that resistance to the Dred Scott decision is "rebellion, treason, and revolution."

The Dred Scott decision did not receive the same reaction in the North. Cries of outrage filled the northern newspapers. Horace Greeley, editor of the *New York Tribune* described the decision as "atrocious, wicked, and abominable." The *Chicago Democratic-Press* expressed a "feeling of shame and loathing." The *Chicago Tribune* was at a loss for words: "We scarcely know how to express our [disgust]."

Northern Republicans claimed that a southern conspiracy existed to make slavery legal throughout the country. In Ohio, the state legislature declared that any slave who entered Ohio would be freed immediately. Justice Curtis was so disappointed with Taney's opinion that he resigned from the Supreme Court.

Horace Greeley was a journalist who was well-known for his antislavery position.

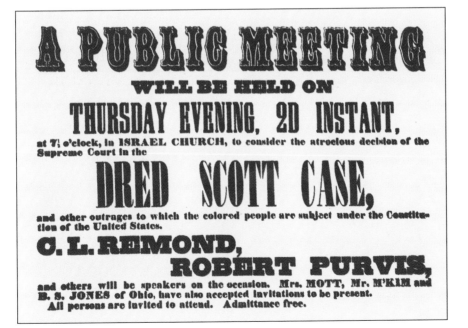

A PUBLIC MEETING
WILL BE HELD ON
THURSDAY EVENING, 2D INSTANT,
at 7½ o'clock, in ISRAEL CHURCH, to consider the atrocious decision of the Supreme Court in the
DRED SCOTT CASE,
and other outrages to which the colored people are subject under the Constitution of the United States.
C. L. REMOND,
ROBERT PURVIS,
and others will be speakers on the occasion. Mrs. MOTT, Mr. M'KIM and B. S. JONES of Ohio, have also accepted invitations to be present.
All persons are invited to attend. Admittance free.

Following the Court's ruling, many northern towns organized public meetings so that citizens could express their anger.

The Dred Scott decision did not achieve Taney's aim to preserve slavery. Instead, Taney drew ferocious criticism. Many northerners believed the decision was a step toward making slavery legal throughout the United States. Anti-slavery feeling throughout the North increased dramatically, and thousands of northerners joined the Republican Party. The reputation of the U.S. Supreme Court was shattered. The slavery issue remained unresolved, and the country drifted closer to civil war.

After the Civil War began in April 1861, President Abraham Lincoln and Republican members of Congress treated the Supreme Court as if it didn't exist. Ignoring Taney's feeble protests, the Republicans abolished slavery from

This law finally abolishing slavery in the state of Missouri was passed only after the Emancipation Proclamation was issued.

all of the western territories in 1862. Later that year, President Lincoln made a decision that surprised even his closest supporters—he issued the Emancipation Proclamation, which freed the slaves and ended slavery in the United States forever. By that time, however, it was too late to help Dred Scott.

In May 1858, Taylor Blow, a descendent of Dred Scott's original owner, Peter Blow, took possession of Scott and his family and set them free. The courageous slave who had fought so long and so hard for his freedom was finally free. Dred, however, could enjoy his freedom for only a short time. He died on September 17, 1858.

Abraham Lincoln was elected the country's sixteenth president in 1860.

This freedom bond, signed by Dred Scott and Taylor Blow, was official documentation that Dred Scott was a free man.

Know all Men by these Presents, That We, _____ as principal, and _____ as securities, are held and firmly bound unto the State of Missouri, in the just and full sum of *Ten* hundred Dollars, lawful money of the United States, for the payment of which we bind ourselves, our heirs, executors and administrators, firmly by these presents, sealed with our seals, and dated this *4* day of *May* A.D. 18*58* The condition of the above Obligation is such, that whereas the said _____ has applied to the County Court of St. Louis County for, and obtained a license to reside in the State of Missouri, during good behavior: Now, if the said applicant shall be of good character and behavior during *his* residence in the State of Missouri, then this obligation to be void, else of full force and virtue.

GLOSSARY

atrocious – extremely cruel or terrible

Capitol – the building where the United States Congress meets

chief justice – leading judge on a court

dissenting opinion – decision that goes against the majority opinion

Justice Curtis wrote the dissenting opinion.

fateful – something that is important because it has a strong and usually unpleasant effect on future events

feeble – very weak

illiterate – not able to read or write

justice – judge who decides court cases

opinion – written document that a judge writes to decide a case and explain the reasoning behind the decision

plantation – large farm that specializes in growing one specific crop

plantation

sue – to take a person to court seeking justice or financial rewards

Supreme Court – highest court in the United States; decides laws that affect all of the states

tactics – methods used to win a battle or achieve a goal

territory – unsettled area that had not yet become a state

treason – to go against one's government

TIMELINE

1800 Dred Scott born

1820 Missouri Compromise

1834 ⎫
1836 ⎬ Emerson and Scott live in Illinois
1837 ⎭ Emerson and Scott live in Wisconsin Territory

Emerson dies **1843**

Scott sues Eliza Emerson for his freedom **1846**

Scott wins; Emerson appeals **1850**

Missouri's highest court rules Scott a slave **1852**

1854 Scott appeals to U.S. Supreme Court

1856 *February 11:* Case begins in Supreme Court

1857

1858 *September 17:* Dred Scott dies

1860 Abraham Lincoln elected president

1861

Civil War ⎰ **1862** Congress bans slavery from territories
1863 Emancipation Proclamation frees slaves
1864 Taney dies
1865

March 6: Taney reads decision

March 7: Curtis reads dissenting opinion

May: Taylor Blow frees Scott family

INDEX (*Boldface page numbers indicate illustrations.*)

PHOTO CREDITS
Photographs ©: AP/Wide World Photos: 17, 31 bottom left; Architect of the Capitol: 18, 31 bottom right; Corbis-Bettmann: 6, 10, 27 top; Missouri Historical Society: cover, 3, 11, 15, 28, 29 bottom, 31 top; North Wind Picture Archives: 1, 4 top, 9, 14, 19, 22, 26; Photri: 23; Stock Montage, Inc.: 2, 4 bottom, 7, 8, 16, 24, 27 bottom, 29 top, 30 bottom; Collection of the Supreme Court of the United States: 20, 25, 30 top; TJS Design: 5, 13.

ABOUT THE AUTHOR
Brendan January was born and raised in Pleasantville, New York. He attended Haverford College in Pennsylvania, where he earned his B.A. in history and English. An American history enthusiast, he has written several books for the Cornerstones of Freedom series including, *The Emancipation Proclamation, Fort Sumter*, and *The Lincoln-Douglas Debates.* Mr. January divides his time between New York City and Danbury, Connecticut.